A CRY FROM THE BLUE

A CRY FROM THE BLUE

SELECTED POEMS
1983 — 1993

SHAUN McCARTHY

5/10 *Shaun McCarthy* [signature]

UNIVERSITY OF SALZBURG
1993

First published in 1993 by Salzburg University in its series:

Salzburg Studies in English Literature
Poetic Drama and Poetic Theory

106

Editor: JAMES HOGG

Academic advisers: HOLGER KLEIN, LEO TRUCHLAR and FRANZ ZAIC
Assistant to the editor: SABINE FOISNER

Copyright © Shaun McCarthy 1994

ISBN: 3 - 7052 - 0636 - 2

Institut für Anglistik und Amerikanistik
Universität Salzburg
A-5020 Salzburg Austria

Distributed in the UK by: Hippopotamus Press, 22 Whitewell Road, Frome, Somerset.

Distributed in the U.S.A. and Canada by: Edwin Mellen Press, 240 Portage Road, Lewiston, New York 14092, U.S.A.

ACKNOWLEDGEMENTS are due to the editors of the following magazines in whose pages some of these poems first appeared: *Acumen, Agenda, Artswest, Bananas, Doors, Dublin Evening Herald, Fatchance, The Green Book, Honest Ulsterman, Interactions, Odyssey, Orbit, Ore, Outposts, Pennine Platform, People to People, Pick, Poetry Durham, Poetry Nottingham, Poetry Review, Present Tense, Quartz, Scripsi, South West Review, Vision On, Westwords.*

'The Ice House' won the *Dublin Evening Herald* Poetry Prize.

CONTENTS

Author's Prolegomenon	ix
Ship In A Bottle	1
Even Now	2
The Ice House	3
On A Coach	4
The Air Farmer	6
A Cry From The Blue	7
Heart Of The House	8
Tyn Church, Prague	10
Bohemian Coronation	12
Family Voices	13
House	14
Stephenson's Axle	16
'Vignette With Picaresque Figures'	17
Outhouse	18
Man With Chicken	19
Black Country	20
Outreach	21
Old Workings, West Cork	22
Holiday Story	24
Dursey Silence	26
An Ornate Wooden House In East Anglia	28
On The Solent	30
Pen And Ink	31
The Wished-For Deer	32
London Churches	34
The Scrapbook Of M. R. James	36
As I Grow Older	37
An Aversion To Flemish Painting	38
The Angler's Dream	39
Traveller	40
Old Men With Boats	41
Woodcut: A Factory Hand, *circa 1770*	42

Aerodrome	44
Travelling Fair	46
Poetry In Schools	47
Geography Of Illusion	48
The Life Of Mirrors	49
Coasting	50
Average Rainfall	51
Wild Geese	52
Rabbit Dusk	53
The World That Day	54
Valediction	55

from *Not Getting On:*

Ruin's Rack (A Sequence)	59
Country Ways (1)	64
Country Ways (2)	65
The Model Village	66
The Last House In The Village	68
Cottage	70
Poet In The Green Estate	71
In The Mushroom Wood	72
Field System	73
Goats	74
The Lonely Girls On Chestnut Horses	76

AUTHOR'S PROLEGOMENON

Most collections of poems are introduced by no more than a couple of quotations whose relevance to the rest of the book is often arcane or otherwise elusive. The poet exists in and through the poems and the reader is not particularly encouraged to learn more about the wider intelligence behind the writing. If the book is a sequence or some other extended piece of verse writing the author may provide some useful background information to the subject and their connection with it, but as most books of poetry are simply, like the first section of this one, an edited collection of poems written over a period of years, this form of exposition of the author's poetic intentions is rare. As so much contemporary verse appears to be at best solipsistic and at worst plain diaristic at the moment, this lack of background is not much of a problem: the poet provides us with a great deal of their own situation, mental and actual (and often rather trivial), in each successive poem. But this form of background does not provide the reader with more than a sort of circumstantial evidence of the poet's own view of their work, their methods and intentions.

And yet is it not the case when one finds a writer whose poems one admires, then the desire to find out more about the author, the broad circumstances within which the poems were written, and perhaps something about the authorial figure themself, soon follows? Thus when asked by James Hogg, editor of this volume, to provide and introduction to the poems gathered here, I was both pleased to be allowed this 'indulgence', and daunted by the prospect of finding something coherent to say about my own writing.

Dr. Hogg asked for something about 'my aims, technique ... and achievement'. The first two I feel comfortable with, and hope the continuing ambitions that have animated these poems and my other writing over the last ten years can be accounted for in some way that will prove helpful to the readers of the poems. As for my 'achievement', others will have to tell! And I must stress that in being allowed space to define a credo, one is not necessarily assuming that one has achieved all the aims stated therein; but I hope that dealing with some of them in this introduction might add something to the reading of the poems that follow.

I find it easier to begin defining what I try to do when I write a poem in terms of what I try to avoid. In 1991 I interviewed Derek Walcott for *Outposts* magazine. During the course of our discussion he spoke of the need for a poet to at least try for some sort of public utterance, whereas it seemed to him that at the moment 'All the poets are retreating into little monasteries where they

Author's prolegomenon

are busy writing their diaristic free verse, saying "I'm not feeling so hot today".'

It seems obvious, on historical evidence if nothing else, that a poet should strive to move from the private experience to the broader public statement. Yet it seems currently fashionable to, as it were, draw up short all the time from completing the second half of this process in any overtly stated way: to regard the perfect lyrical observation as one which holds back from developing the personal event into something more specifically formulated, more enduring and of wider relevance. Seemingly almost fearful of proposing an argument or stating a case beyond the particular circumstances of the subject of the poem, and their emotive response to it, so many writers seem to leave the reader with no more than a well-turned sense of irony as the final translation of their personal experience expressed through the poem.

In most of the poems in this collection I have tried to move as clearly as possible from the particular to the universal; even if, at the least ambitious level, that universal is only a sharing, through a sort of crystallisation, of the essence of a quite ordinary experience. More often though I try to look at the circumstances that create the situations which we encounter in our lives: be these social, physical or internally generated. To that extent there is a deliberate tendency for some of the poems to be slightly didactic in their concluding lines. I do not find it enough to create an almost blank space for the reader to develop their own subsequent thoughts after the poem's conclusion; I would like to try for rather more control over the final impact that reading a poem has. Of course, it is the nature of poetry that the final interpretation will be influenced by the intelligence, feelings and particular situation of the individual reader, but I would like to think that they are all moved by the poem in roughly the same direction.

I attend a lot of poetry readings and find that many quite successful performing poets work from an essentially diaristic subject base; and through the quotidian, domestic focus of their poems readily engage the audience. The most usual response to their work is a mild laugh at the irony which they employ to draw out, with not too much seriousness, something underlying the event they describe, combined with a low chuckle of recognition. I don't think this is enough: I do not imagine this is ultimately a meaningful response to art, nor in anything but the short term, a satisfying one for either poet or reader.

As a writer, I would at least hope to draw more than this sort of response from an audience or a reader. The danger is that to seek to do more than work within this fashion of wry lyricism often feels like swimming against a current, and that to try to direct the reader or audience towards some more analytic

Author's prolegomenon

conclusion may raise accusations of self-righteous polemic. From this, the cry of 'boredom' quickly follows. But I would rather risk boring an audience trying to say something that I think matters and has more than casual relevance, than to simply succeed in amusing them. So these poems are not designed to amuse! However, I would hope that in the scope of their subject matter (not their themes), starting points that are domestic in many cases, a reader might find things that touch on their daily experience. But that experience of recognition, of our commonalty, is only intended as a basis for moving forward towards a theme.

What then might these themes typically be? Leaving aside the poems in the second section of this book, which were designed to form a loose but constantly focused whole, what are the concerns that I find myself returning to? I have to say that any consideration of recurring themes can only be stated in general terms. I do not write my poems to an ordered plan: there is not, for example, a definite political motive through which I consistently interpret my personal experiences.

I am certainly interested in the presence of social and historical universals in what may, on the surface, appear to be the most personal and unique private experience. Moving from an evocation of an event, scene or experience, through which I try to recreate for the reader the emotions that surround it, I try to provide and develop my own account of the reasons, causes, consequences or whatever, of the subject. There are, therefore, almost two parts to many of the poems: the reviving of a common memory, experienced by poet and hopefully recalled in their own version by the reader, moving on to my own development of some more thematic facet contained within that experience. To this second, more constructed, phase, the reader's response can, of course, vary; from agreement to total rejection of my version of what underlies or follows on from the starting point. Poems are not theorems of course, and these separate elements are variously interwoven, merged and just plain hard to find in many of the poems! Nonetheless, although even such a general statement of intent or method as this seems to over-state what the poems themselves contain, this is the broad intention behind the conception of many of them, and the process by which I attempt to execute them. I hope they succeed; and in ways more organic and certainly less mechanical than the terms in which I have spoken of them here.

My first collection, a pamphlet from Hippopotamus Press, was entitled *Places* because, as a very young writer, I was concerned with the idea of the spirit of place as a subject for (largely descriptive) poetry. I suspect that this sort of verse, particularly if the places that engage the poet are rural, is not

Author's prolegomenon

generally considered (perhaps for very good cultural reasons) as being at the cutting edge of contemporary verse. I do not think I am being over-sensitive when I say that the term 'nature poet' is often tinged with a certain dismissiveness nowadays. But I am still interested in the power of words to evoke the spirit of place, and as the place where I live and write is rural, many of my poems at least begin in rural locations. Making these vivid to readers, and looking into some of the dynamics, natural and human, that create the spirit of place there, is still one of my recurring concerns 'Where can we live but days?' said Philip Larkin; and as we all move endlessly through a continuum of not only time but also space, then where else can we live but the place we inhabit? Using descriptive images of the physical world as a way into the essential contract of communication between writer and reader seems to me a device that is immediately useful. No matter how internalised or abstract the theme of a poem, I like to anchor it with a subject that is part of the 'real world' as far as possible. Evoking a commonly experienced sense of place can also be an end in itself, but I hope that in these poems the reader can share in the move from this sort of evocation into something more analytic and abstract.

Most of the poems in the section entitled 'Not Getting On' attempt to work in this way, though they are driven by a desire not merely to re-draw the comfortable image of British rural life so much as to present the less attractive side of the psychology that life-long struggle in such an environment can create. During the period when these were written there was a lot of popular interest in the notion of the rural way of life as re-discoverable and desirable to a largely urban population in the UK. Living in the country I was both pleased by the favourable interpretation of country images on a conservation level, but also repeatedly struck by the gross over-simplification of the country-side and its rural communities, at least as I was experiencing living in one. Although working from particular personal impressions (chiefly of Somerset in England and, rather less darkly, the west coast of Ireland), I hope the overall import of the poems builds to some sort of more public statement.

The villages described are actual locations in the South West of England, and the events in 'Ruins Rack' are quite closely based on two famous cases of suicide pacts among the members of inbred and isolated farming families. I have tried to paint a picture of the lives that ended in such 'stalled places' without involving the names and details specifically. I hope that a degree of universality is thus created which would not be possible if I had simply dramatised a specific set of tragic events. And I hope I have avoided any sense of undue voyeurism: the 'picturesque rustic' has been mythologised, sanitized and completely removed from social realism for long enough, in English verse in particular. His fictional alter-ego, the suspicious and curmudgeonly tenant

Author's prolegomenon

of an inevitable ramshackle and embattled holding, can equally easily be removed from reality. I hope the cast of 'Ruin's Rack' do not appear as rustic grotesques: to portray them in such a way was never my intention.

Returning to the notion of defining what I have attempted to do over the last ten years of writing in terms of what I do not do, I would like to take some space to briefly consider the metrical structure of the poems. I undertake a lot of reviewing for various small magazines, and read a lot of contemporary poetry besides for pleasure. Increasingly I find myself unable to locate in much of what I read even the basic dynamics of the poetic nature of the language employed. Charged with defining poetry by means of the particulars of the language it employs, as distinct from its normal prosaic use, I find myself unable sometimes to see even what general principles the poets, of what they would, no doubt, claim to be 'free verse', are employing. I am not by any means denying the importance of free verse in saying this. I see free verse as a logical development in many writers' work, and of the tradition of verse writing (following on from Modernism) generally. But in those free verse poems which I admire one is constantly struck somehow by a sense of linguistic order and purpose, of the poet knowing what traditional metrical rules they are moving away from, and why they are choosing to work in a free verse way.

But so often it seems I come across poems for which I cannot identify any critical values by which to judge or make sense of the structure, or its apparent total lack. And for myself I find the attraction of rhyme and rhythm increasingly powerful. Generally speaking the poems in this collection that employ end rhyme or fairly strict metrical line length, etc. are the later pieces. I suspect my future output will be all end rhymed.

There are many personal reasons for this, and I must point out that I am advocating not general rules to which I think all poets should subscribe, but merely accounting for my own private preferences and aspirations. I have always felt that whatever else a poet may be, he or she should strive to make memorable phrases. And for me memorable phrases seem to be those where the rhythm, and often the accompanying rhyme, creates a pattern that facilitates the memorising of the lines and underscores with a certain musicality the meaning contained in the words. One of the greatest powers of poetry, of any era, is the ability it has to be resonant. For me, much of this resonance comes from the rhythm within which the words and the poet's intelligence are contained. And I find it simply more enjoyable to read aloud poems which have a strong metrical urge to them. Even on the page a uniform structure seems to me something pleasing to work towards. Almost all of these poems

Author's prolegomenon

are in stanzas composed of equal numbers of lines, or in a pattern of alternating numbers of lines. I think the poems lie more attractively on the page if so structured: and it seems to me to be one of the required basic skills of a poet to be able to sort their thoughts into metrically coherent units.

Indeed the demands of even quite plain metrical structures are opportunities: for testing one's poetic discipline and for looking for ways to revive and personalise poetic devices that have been employed (for very good reasons) for often hundreds of years. Perhaps I am not a sufficiently inspired or experimental metrician, but I need to have a very strong reason for abandoning the general poetic practices that have been employed and refined for centuries. In those places where I have worked in a manner more akin to free verse, I have usually done so because I felt the subject was best served by this approach, and usually settled on this only after trying more metrically formal versions.

Shaun McCarthy

Ruett Farm
Somerset

18.10.1993

SHIP IN A BOTTLE

I am the skipper
of a ship in a bottle,
a flashy trick
on a sunlit bar.

But long smoky hours
have swallowed my set,
this pint of oceans,
south seas blue,

mats to gummy brown;
sad as the shells
with no echo left
bedded in villa paths.

No bluster on my
dusty quarter deck,
my course is set
to the glass dead-end

Fish eyes squinny
at the trick of masts;
like love in a dumb
mouth my cry, "Ahoy,"

is a stoppered O.
This bottle's a sea
with no floor, no rest,
though bells ring Time—

Trapped like a genie
on my Marie Celeste
by wax and cotton
and an old hand's knack.

EVEN NOW
'Even now there are places where a thought might grow'
DEREK MAHON.

Where thought might grow; become the place of spirits,
which place creates, in local god's own image;
where time can tune, finer than any mind,
the fixed intent of inanimate things,
where every molecule is focused to
the steady airstream in a tumbled drift

and rock shrieks in its water torture.
The gentle tipping mill bears down each crack
the last worked ounce of its cantilever—
These precincts are for gods whose slow collapse
restores them to a pre-industrial ease.

Where space enough lies void and soiled with work—
Not emblematic miles-from-anywheres:
saintly desert columns, harsh extremes,
not aching to be famous calms of light
and cabins trimmed for crews discovered gone;
but local mysteries of ownerships

where moisture rubs the rule of thumb
from things put briefly down and left for years,
where ghost hands work across a rotting bench
and the last volt sighs in a battery.
Where a thought might grow, to be itself a place.

THE ICE HOUSE

She fears her lady's cartomancy
and the tinker's boy who called with knives,
then at dinner the master roars
for ice and she is sent

beyond soft lawns chevroned with light
along blind walks of yew to steps
that sink to nightmares, dormant chills
and impish percolations

that mark remote, unworldly time.
Her lantern swoons in the dome's embrace,
her steps place someone opposite
behind the glowing berg.

She scoops and flies, the clanging door
calls her name but she is gone
a moth to the light of rebukes
and chores; until next time.

Condemned to return, she is consoled
by knowing where fear, like ice, must stay;
and sure she has no leisure for cards,
and nothing that tinkers steal.

ON A COACH

We were running East, and night rushed on;
estuarine sky's pale navigations,
earth-bound lamps configurations,
out-shone landscape's softer glow.

I was riding in the front seat
on the panoramic upper deck,
dazed by the crawl-to-sudden-dash
of blinding traffic streaming past:

but as we skimmed beneath a bridge
its span of lights went out; then sparks
of speeding dazzle changed into dark,
quick as a switch: and last, our own

now pioneering beams snapped off.
Motion vanished, engine's hum
and the rustle and buffet of wind were gone;
all in such order as though some hand

moved on a console, closing down ...
everything. I was small as a bird
stilled by a blackness beyond words.
And then there was nothing left to think;

except "This is like death," which is
not a journey on through warnings,
changed perceptions, mute surroundings;
not a "Would you now get off

this commandeered "bus?" and a tap on the arm
from a gaunt conductor strict as a bell—
And the only shame was I could not tell
anyone else how sad it was;

that it is nowhere and nothing—Yet
something inside has the last act:
like an after image, I clearly felt
the unseen light in myself go out.

THE AIR FARMER

The farmer of the future breathes
his own success, his herd
of photosynthesising conifers
nod grave heads like good cattle.

Paid to farm air, no roaring saw
chips these ponderous ariel sighs;
filaments in an acreage
of verdant lung, reviving the breeze

that sweeps them into motion as if
they breathed like humans. Earth's damp
and the odour of greenness is thick:
the oxygen level soars and streams

away in unmeasured value, paid
by airy height, to keep alive
a world that's choked on shimmering fuel.
Down alleys forbidden to walkers,

on forest floors too deep for soil
to bear a plant, the farmer moves
like a particle inside a lung,
whistling profitable wind.

A CRY FROM THE BLUE

It was the middle afternoon,
hot and stinging, when suddenly
there was a cry from the blue,

grounded in no one place.
The field beyond the hedge was still,
nothing slipped round the green corner

and all points held the slight
surprise of inanimate objects
disturbed, in their essence, by humans.

Was it a call of warning
to a stealthy second that I was there,
crouched in the fuss of a stalled mower?

It was hard to say even if
human or creature voiced the syllable—
It was not god-like, certainly.

A simple cry from the blue, except
that field, lane and hedge were blank
as tape that awaits the press of sound;

a cry portentous as the tile
that falls in a dead calm, the pile
of books that crash in an empty room.

HEART OF THE HOUSE

Cornered on tiles in the deepest room
I am cold hearted; vitreous sheen
out-shone by August's window show.

My red skin burns with rust, dust
and birdsong congeal in my throat.
My belly is an uncleared meal.

The household gods are all outdoors:
stretched like a cat, all windows wide,
the farm basks at the striped lawn's end,

is prized for its shade, rich walls of fruit,
gathered and cut and brighter than me
on cold dishes that win applause.

>But when the first disfocussed dusk
>shows visible breath, then I am stirred,
>the thin draught in my blackened throat,

>an air-stream in a mine's clogged drift,
>is struck into life. Thick as an engine,
>my chest will take all night to warm

>and my long continuous exhalation
>rolls up into the frosted sky.
>The village is plumed like a fleet at rest

>moonlit in a dead, cold calm. Talk
>round various fires is of logs
>and draughts. I am praised again.

>>If I could reproduce myself
>>I would melt the hearts of furnaces
>>to forge my saurian bars and plates

and boil them into living things
as I now am live. Summers
are parabolic: I am cast.

Throned in a web of lulling pipes,
crowned by pots that feed and bloat,
I imagine flinching trees, shrunk

curlicues of outdoor iron.
Roaring wood applauds me, hands
reach out, and palm age-old respect.

TYN CHURCH, PRAGUE

Behind the ill-hung door with coffin trims
gothic and baroque entwine like vines
or cave secretions racked to human form
Goya-esque and plagued by seraphim
hung like bats around gaunt martyrs' crowns.

Outside, new pilgrims muster unruly packs,
the bright and bored school trips that fidget round
a thronged square's novelties. But ushered in
from sunlight, crowding bleak isles, they draw back
as sibilance like vertigo hushes them.

The dead might spring from stage traps out of crypts
where Tycho Brahe, noseless as a saint,
disfigures dust this shuffling damage sifts.
But if memento mori seal their lips,
their jokes and irritated guides, or if

half-purged familial priest-fear herds them, fenced
beyond the piercing glare of statuary,
or if only boredom rears in this absurd
sepulchral concourse, I'm not sure, but sense
that some thing not quite properly preserved

should move us more than to a carcass feast.
The pious stone men round this vault seem lost
in broken peace and unattended bells.
The trips retreat, cowed as though ill-dressed,
needing a half-brave face, despite themselves,

to turn away from something so obviously meant,
but farcical and chill. A dead man pinned
to building wood and flecked with gouts like rain
shocks any eye that moves and grows in light,
which looks for windows, finds them flush with pain

and every fresco, tablet, shade of night
commends us to a beauty through duress,
repels these young, troubles my penance to art.
The world rejoined seems freer, teems with light
from sky new-made of limitless clear air.

BOHEMIAN CORONATION

The young man is arranged for this
and enters from spring light
cool vaults that momentarily appal;

footings among the bones of those
who named this stony right:
to never fully leave again these walls.

Coined power, from which the basilica grows,
will trophy him in art:
his image will become impersonal rule.

And now he leaves, sealed rings are kissed,
this puppy must learn to bite
and find all wishes run upon his call.

He'll die in harness, however long the reign:
such absolute life; such sudden death in all.

FAMILY VOICES

These women exhausted by children
keep hours I do not know. School
reveilles wring their days.

It begins with breaking of quiet,
end in words for what should be
fingers to lips, the drift to sleep.

What human ebb dries these faces,
then covers them wet again? How
do they keep it up? Each is a grain

of sand in an oyster house made loud
with cries for elbow room—
I need furniture's polished tongues.

Yet am I ignorant, will find
I should have registered brief life
as most do in regeneration

that will be them in part, and where
quiet times will ring with voices' second
story; while I will simply die?

No small hand ever held mine, though I
have cradled a dear, dying animal;
and lived whole days without words.

HOUSE
(Being restored in Co. Westmeath.)

The house woke in every window
flung up to throw out dust, bring in
resinous new timber. Men came
who knew the ways of stone and wood
to make again the signs of grace.

They banged old door like boxes,
brewed tea with a kettle on the boards,
began work of stripping back
to bring to light the plasterer's tired
mistake of a long day lifetime's ago;

cutting down, through patterns, motifs,
the undated papers whose age is guessed
by news, through changeable fashions of gloss
scorched to a blur beneath their flames;
until the rightness of proportions

exposed its walls like ancient skin.
They were ready to begin, conferred
on ragging, marble, re-learned effects
of affluent harmony to ghost
original hands—They never could;

any more than the local teenager
tricked out in formal black and white
who will serve on certain evenings here
could ever be a servant girl.
The lamp had long ceased to burn

by which the welcome in these crafts
could shine through unlit countryside.
There was nothing left for them to make
but artifice and make-believe—
It did not blaze like this when new,

their work lights burned unshaded glass:
though viewed, they only saw themselves
in dark, untroubled grounds that hid
the grace which finally fled, restored
its fine decay and mocked their care

with line and rule—The garden stayed
alive, while all the house fell dead.
The craftsmen revved and bolted, left
a fire of broken scrap, the home
which lived and made decline its own.

STEPHENSON'S AXLE

Did they know the world would change?
Sunlight in pillars in worksheds off
the beaten, yet to be laid tracks.
Parts whose pattern bemused their maker
slip into place to synchronise
some point in history's patent book
where talent, need and luck combine.

An apprentice or casual hand is sent
to find, say, an axle beam;
some other purposed, random length;
and coming back with make-do binds
the globe to never meeting lines
four feet, eight and a half inches apart—
The arbitrary is fathomless.

Our lives, too, just fall to hand:
a chance joy, a start in a far
town, become both love and home.
Where else might we be? with whom?
had not two journeys met on lines,
the standard gauge of parallels,
which met in a sense: perspective's trick.

'VIGNETTE WITH PICARESQUE FIGURES'

The long evening of a golden age
when revels wait upon the door
of a galleon-timbered room to throw
the artist springing from his labours
into the visible bosom of friends,
and his keen, more sociable graces.

It is Sheridan, released
from his locked room by a last act;

it is a circumnavigator
many-armed with furling maps.

The simple rewards, lewd and rumpled:
pewter and linen and heavy chairs
pushed from the table. Pamphlets and play-bills
have their proponents. The studded door
bursts in again and gentlemen-thieves
swirl their cloaks like Jesuit spies.

It is a beauty got up as a footpad
whose sex will be made weak tonight;

it is a wind blown without quarter
bringing the curtain down in fright.

OUTHOUSE

The world is so much patchwork, leaning-to;
drab places between perfects where we live
the rusty boundaries where rights slip through,
adapted, gimcrack, cobbled up to give

some use, to one who has no further use.
So we inherit all the making-do
and botch our own, re-stacking shrinking space:
in time tar-paper patches up the view

and every mended thing gives up its ghost,
lies welded by decay into a reef
of ferrous coral, verdigrised and choked:
thus plots thicken, leaf on brittle leaf,

and in each sagging glory-hole dim rows
of seized-up mechanisms drop apart
to dog the backyard Michelangelos
whose makeshift visions failed both science and art.

Whole countries are allotments, from the air,
going to weed; in sheds where light remains
armies of bodgers solder on, repair
the fits and starts that once were grand designs.

MAN WITH CHICKEN

Might be a Dadaist caption
for grounded mechanical forms:
in fact a simple pastoral,
man on one knee, his best hen attending.

Both creatures are butts
of knockabout comedy, both on occasion
furies of dust and rancour
wheeling in clockwork frustration.

Man and his good layer,
the chain of dependence is short as a fetter.
Dusk is settling grain by grain,
eggs are scattered, the fox awake.

But here is great ease,
a hand lying slack against the knee,
her claw half raised. The man
reflects and the hen has her thoughts.

BLACK COUNTRY

This was built to intimidate,
windows to angle out ghastly faces
gas-raw in attic redoubts
that blacken the sky, that confiscate
like school dormers weak light of day
admitted too high for shadow play.

The wings of terminal wards, of courts,
of steam-engined companies, franchises
on empires ages past cashed in.
Names founded in brick exhort
with classical fonts their date and grace;
calligraphy soot-shading into trace.

Impossible to grasp the will
that raised such gothic over-worlds
on a blank sheet, on plain fields
to clothe disdain for human scale.
Tall doors swallowed apprentice voices
into sibilence and workroom places.

Who, with a pen commissioned to draw
cottage or tenement close, would choose
gloom from daylight, tiled wall from hedge?
Unless the age demanded more
than greed determined: uniform to hide
like the body itself, life's human side.

In gutters below the highest crags
of confined windows pigeons flirt
like mad hands scratching at moss.
Roof weeds like pennants, ivy swags
in time would hang Babylonian green,
or fall to earth with the wrecker's chain.

OUTREACH

Like haywire radios
their static voices
rarely serve a full sentence.

From smuggled overhearings
on their dial's edge
they have locked on simple phrases,

all slightly out of date.
"Here comes trouble,"
"I know a thing or two,"

and "You'd forget your head"
are quip and tick
to stir exaggerated fuss,

with hands that flutter in mock
balletic foldings.
Limbs won't quite support

the body's argument
with itself,
its onward lurching hunch.

They are hard repetitive work
but always gentle:
I have 'to count to ten.'

And when, five times, they want
"Your guts for garters,"
they don't; but need your hands.

OLD WORKINGS, WEST CORK

Where a sheep's step might open turf
and the white cage of bones be found
a season after,

where the seam descends out of plumb
slant-wise into the water-clock
of the earth's pocket,

where the rare curious pebble lobbed
by a cautious, softly-treading walker
sometimes finds

lodging a few feet under the lip
sometimes the centre shaft, imagine
what stirrings then

in the black slash under midday sun,
in the still presence of men for whom
these galleries

were a neighbourhood through the bitten hill
with corners, meetings, unsound places;
daylight a dream.

Talk in the bars is of land-work and fishing,
nothing's been mined since '22
and the owner shot

on his castle drive in the civil war.
The quarries from which that pile was shaped
were open to weather

as the house is now, its shell rinsed
of the gothic scorch of floors and rafters,
of a night as black

as underground, when through the park
where shrubs were craggy as rock the gang
of shifty torches came.

HOLIDAY STORY

The softest country in County Cork
folds around Ilen's tidal stream,
everything curved like a celtic torque
enamelled by mud as the river dries.

We set up camp on a grass-topped pier:
on the farther bank a by-road squeezed
the ebbing reach. Then a salmon
arched in the shallows, ripples showed

not tranquil depths but rocks beneath
the surface stretched and shrinking fast.
A plastic crate rolled by, beached
as corners grounded on the bed.

Herons and other long-beaks settled,
poised camera ready, took the bank
like anglers in a gala. Fish
jumped more frantically now, broke

where their chances shrank. Beaks stabbed,
throats sword-swallowed. Under a hoarding
on the by-road extolling a traffic scheme,
under the sweeping Georgian gaze

of a white house used to quiet afternoons,
this daily slaughter ran, fish seeking
ever more shallow, serpentine routes,
birds wading in, wings moving

quick as shutters. How thin the roof
of water and safety must seem
from inside the river, grim proof
of the force that sends the salmon here,

by sun and moon this must run on,
such decimation, such silvered flood
consumed that some, god knows, must turn
upstream again on the next brief tide.

There is nothing to say, but that this happens,
completes some feral balancing act
from which the soul seems absent; patterns
of need and statistical fact.

Darwinian luck or convenient chance
makes our higher condition trite and free,
unfolds no wings above our journey,
no drive but our own itinerary.

On another face of this gentle globe
bombers are stitching a cemetery
of crosses to the sky, the road
they dive upon some flooded by-way

breaking like water, where the test of flesh
is that the winged shapes cannot feed
on what they kill, that on some point
of indifference a camp dines out.

DURSEY SILENCE

On greasy hawsers we swing across,
a simple cupboard latch fidgets
to keep out singing Atlantic winds.

The cable car yaws like a heavy tub,
clear of the rocks its shadow is lost
in water stiffened to blue matt.

We land on broken concrete,
a wave to the mainland triggers off
the last chance to leave tonight.

Silence. The island's different
though moored to the car-dotted opposite coast.
Wind through heather, a sheep's step

are tuned and distinct; seals at the base
of breathless cliffs make slap-dash din.
This is how it must have sounded

before wires set millions of speakers dancing
and air above roads grew blue with rush.
We are like city people seeing

a clear night from a moor, amazed
at the endless business of stars.
This silence is spacious as the dusk

and full of sound: of drying sand,
feathers' ruffling, my pocket watch
distinct as an insect: irritating.

A silence you could gather up,
and if you spilled it would not make
a drop of sound. The cables are earthed.

NOTE: Dursey Island is sparsely inhabited and connected to the very end of the Beara Peninsula, West Cork, by cable car.

AN ORNATE WOODEN HOUSE
IN EAST ANGLIA

Their house was summer's pavilion,
riverboat balconies stacked towards sea
whose waves were never so cloud white
as ornate boards, and always
calm and even as a blazer's stripes.

They owned the entire sandy point
in a simple, under-stated way:
in games had need of all of it.
For them the lighthouse was mere confection,
the chilly tides always right for a swim.

Occasional gusts snapped at their awnings
and wicker creaked around early teas
when rain stopped play, but every lamp
carried to dinner burned steadily.
It should all have blown away, but

assumed instead its exposed position
with hardly a ruffled edge; serving,
reflecting the class that called and played
the elaborate rituals of the house.
After the colonies, this was peace.

It took the slow intrusion
of small black cars, stray violations,
couples at night and caravans
to break the spell which kept them sure.
As kings are dumb when subjects turn

away to their own concerns, the house
was wide open less and less; sunsets
glowed on unvisited beds. Now storms
may run their course, sea revise
the coast where posts slip under floods;

and if whatever the frivolous house
encouraged in voices from open windows
was arrogance and privilege,
or whether it mattered that shingles held
crisp and remarkable against gales

that drive the trippers into gloom
and rooms without initiative,
I do not know; but more is lost
than laughter at cards on wet afternoons
in the house where surprise was expected.

ON THE SOLENT

Though they review the spotless yachts
in a view they tend like a window box,
had they still legs for sea they'd chose the
placid lines of a motor cruiser

and brief afternoons. Their white and blue
apartments smell of builder's work and, through
double-glass, of stale sun's cure—
What they've kept decks out a life of leisure.

In tidy garages newly lettered
modest saloons gather sand and light.
Their outgoings are small: the links, the parks,
the same parade of windswept glass

where girls so like their own are kind
but stay one season. Now short of wind
behind incongruous wrought-iron work they face
the gales that flay this fair-weather friend of a place.

And the sea's elliptical pendulum
grinds at the salt rim of tedium.
Their busy daughters warned of exile
where views become cosmetic as smiles.

PEN AND INK

The uncorrected stick
bends through water's skin,
a pen to write a life
flowing truth and trick.

As memory is threaded
from poor bits snagged on wire,
garnered evidence
of where the flock was led,

so that sand scriber dives
but always slants awry
from quite the bottom point,
from ideas fixed as stones.

The hand above these lines
is full of its own ghosts,
each precursory shade
corporeal and confined.

Required to make ends rhyme
words follow on like sheep;
the bright linguistic bell
shivers to curfew's chimes.

Bell-notes over water,
symbols of time and flux;
and stick or pen's a stylus
dipped out of air sounds into

the steadying deeper drift.
In ink as pure the nib
would show, refracted,
but angled to resist.

THE WISHED-FOR DEER

Misty rain weighs evergreen,
earths the silence, suspends in a drop
all movement of a hemmed-in scene

at whose far end, in a forest ride,
two deer, already arcs in the air,
take flight perfectly side by side

leaving us to fill this raw
enclosed quarter mile of grazing. Shadowy,
half-balletic, half in terror,

their pale rumps flash under boughs:
the escape made in total silence.
Nothing subsides, no warning cries

or stirring hooves; they were like stray
frames in a film. My dog tunes
his whiskery nerves at other prey.

I almost think I wished them here,
and closing on their vanishing point
find high-strung wire barbed and clear,

dense trunks like catacombs beyond.
This wood is a planted factory:
gates are chained, the treeline's bland,

the air of watching ownership lends
a human agency. Sometimes
there's gunfire, flash of binocular lens.

But let there be deer, silent, unculled,
locally precious as a pure well,
as clear sea in a secret cove,

surprising the village and owned land,
their presence a test we cannot make
that something wild and frail can stand.

In deeper chambers of the wood,
bass-toned and crackling like underbrush,
stags clamour for their strayed world.

LONDON CHURCHES

The shock-waved pointillist
of traffic barraged trees
clears to stony dead-fall,
calm blocks of yard and square

sealed in the absence of service;
yet here the gate through iron,
each crack in the right of way,
leads straight to flight underground,

or rather say below
this current surface, pavement
overlays mosaic,
in pits of clay new sites

break into vaults and every
wall and footing is party:
one side computers fathom,
ten feet away through tile
and lime plague dead sink down.

The church bricks up its court;
sounds that start from steps
stop at its blind back wall,
high windows green as silt.

Brass sights and men with canes
drew down the golden rules
not this alchemical dark.
There was form, alignment, pride,
close packed; commissions rose

in rank, and rise up still.
Misuse was known from the start,
where work was dedicated
to odd-named city corners,

where a smoky afternoon
stained new stone like soot,
and the not invented roar
like traffic passed their ears.
Now timelessly ragged tramps

frizzled by lying close
to the church's stone reactor
know dark's a dangerous hour
and feel the dead grow warm.

THE SCRAPBOOK OF M. R. JAMES

A local tragedy, half-confided,
a grain of truth in a sack of ash:
the traveller boards by the winter shore,
the boots is phlegmatic; it's happened before.

A haunting where one should not be found,
behind the rood, or on bleak ground;
the figure in the last train down,
the ugly villa on the edge of town.

A fateful collusion of name and date,
a nocturne whose image revises itself:
absence, the flawless vacancy
of stairs; the twilit ambulatory:

as if a building had quit its plot
or a key unlocked a child-ghost's cot;
linen pursuers wrapped over and over,
clothes taken life opposed to their owner.

Cool erudition, each term correct
for holy office, gothic effect:
his horrors like mottoes old families can't shed,
the open eye in the opposite bed.

AS I GROW OLDER

As I grow older I write about gardens:
the ivy is covering over the house,
lights go on and off at settled times.

I will not change the world, but I can
direct the pattern of green things,
eat the simple fruits of my choice—

Or sometimes, rooting wildness out,
trace the tabby paths that wind
to eyes I do not recognise;

come home in the slack reach of the day
to evidence of the neighbour's sly
incursions; witness unseasonable heat

at noon thrumming on thumb-high shoots:
sky like a white fire drained
of smoke; child and bird song stifled.

And I think "This is life, my life,
proceeding without me." This is how
my body operates: flourishing,

shrivelling. Here the carelessly gathered
cornucopia tumbles; here the thief
and stray slip by—Here I die.

AN AVERSION TO FLEMISH PAINTING

Fish-varnish. Tones of dock water,
palettes of pickling liquor.
Lips for a conference of low sounds:
drainage, pump and sluice.
Introduce a pineapple
or sudden coruscation
to refine the murky table
and fug in the submarine room
would lour fathoms deep.

Stool-sitters. Drinkers from pots
feasting on raw shoals.
Skin tones of cold water bathers.
Their land is sea-floor level,
the rigging of wind pumps
and cantilevered bridges
rocking like dull clocks.
Rustics in diver's footwear
anchor to frugal polders.

Gutturals. Flemish and Walloon;
their leaden plosives suit
breeds of heavy, draught stock; swamp
any more enticing name.
But see this beauty curled, capped,
who lights a bigger scene,
bringing a pineapple-faceted lamp
through barge-black gloom. Some foreign wife?
The artist's child, in fact and face.

THE ANGLER'S DREAM

At dusk the river inverted itself;
the flow steadied, the under-ripple
corrugated a muddy sky.
Corpulent fish passed like golems.

I was miming pebbles of cold air,
rain pocked the water's roof;
twigs descended, dipped into focus.
Fat as sows, the ghost-fish nuzzled.

I knew I was drowned. When the arch
with lights and voices righted itself
I came up for water, not breath.
Fat as a catch, I spread my arms.

TRAVELLER

*'(His) preferred form of travel was to lie on a
divan and have the scenery carried past him.'*
            MAXIME DU CAMP on FLAUBERT.

He woke in a seat,
remembered he was travelling,
and through the window of the bus
swept a widening plain

where good custom prospered
with profit harmonised with charm;
a land of happy families
where shouldered children waved from gates.

For hours, it seemed, he passed
attended fields, towns of local stone;
none familiar, none uninviting:
at any he could alight—

But he journeyed on;
dozing, waking to equable scenes
that he knew would unroll forever,
and he would come to hate.

OLD MEN WITH BOATS

I envy the old men with boats spending days
galoshing in moats around their careening.

Their studies are acrid net-festooned bars,
their tumble home cabins are lined with knots.

They have smuggled surprising skills, one
serves gumbos richer than a creole chef's,

another can fashion delicate toys
in brown and gold fingers like tangled rope.

Ashore they are awkward as crabs, pushing
decrepit cycles from chandler's to slip.

They rarely put to sea; on stormy
nights they drink after hours with a widow.

They shrug off handsome unseasonable tans;
laugh in the mornings to chase away Death.

WOODCUT: A FACTORY HAND
Circa 1770

Dimly as lessons recalled this man is inked:
calves as slender as a girl, both hands
around the plain shaft of a kite-shaped spade
on which he leans, fatigued, or as required.
         His clay pipe and slouch hat suggest leisure,
though the wider scene is bleak, all curls
of smoke above scoured earth and out-sized wheels,
iron curlicues that brace a hand-turned crane.

He presents more farmer's boy than factory hand:
the master tried to show exactly this
I now suppose, how early mill and forge
grew rustically by water, forest coal,
on tracts where towns weren't. Beyond my school
the purpose of land has long been overlaid
by roofscape, metro lines and factories
like windowed hulls docked on arterial roads.

Now more in light I've read enough to trace
a filled canal across a grazing plain,
know those arches almost blind with earth
as stoke-holes of a charcoal forge, that this
deer-shadowed valley smelted, beat and flared.
I know a cold plantation and a drift
deep within where coal draught vents a shaft,
stones have no echo and under soil is slag.

Men beyond my school life wore the grey
of their war-surviving city, but the man
in the woodcut seemed to have a home among hills
and a width to his sleeves faintly cavalier.
         I vaguely dated Acts drummed out to free
a few of his poor hours from the shaking mill,

and caught the Quaker sentiments that spoke
to give back childhood, safety and good air.

The factory as estate, the village turned
from outwork to a circle round new tools
and guild-like work lofts with a human scale
might illustrate prospectus for a trade
which raised a crop on classic river banks,
set men to patent engines deft and swift,
whose products bettered fashion, staunched the sick,
yielded nothing war-like, were worked up

in manufacturies astride clear streams
from which no drop was drawn nor dregs thrown in—
The cotton trade: whose white threads bound the limbs
of naked Africa, caught slavery's wind,
in prison mills below the drizzled moor
deafened the woman and placed her child beneath
the pinching loom to garner and inhale.
This is the reward of part-learnt history:

knowledge enough to weave two meanings from
a woodcut of a place new-made, or spoiled,
now sunk to rubble in a dappled calm
where ghost hands rock the shadows of a loom.
      The clock of falling masonry's wound down,
and a race like endless blank tape runs too swift
for hours of labour that wore out by shifts
the man with scarecrow calves and an awkward spade.

AERODROME

The shock of the new run to seed:
a biplane's sedentary putter
ruffles the limits of bending grass.

The injured field, long out of lease,
rusts to easy means of trespass,
sags beneath the sprawl of slung

old carpets, baths and tile. The few
unbroken frames in the flying club
harbour the swarthy, goggled face

of a grounded leather man, whose last
round echoes through scrambled rooms.
He molests our sudden isolation

at a point of departure off the map:
the roar of Imperial Lines reduced
to a flapping tune, creaky as wicker,

served up by stewardly nostalgia.
Beneath the weather's dismal dance
black oil bleeds from a Pegasus

and crew in gabardines stand by
as 'good sorts' and their silky wives
tread lightly into empty skies

The long afternoons were blue and tall,
the black-out nights stitched with scores,
cross over cross on the roaring dark,

and pioneering, melting airmen
gauntlet in glove with lost aviatrix
vanished through their soaring gauge,

long overdue from fields like this,
beside unseeing roads, far out
among the red-brick scrub of things,

the haunt of glass-eyed leather men
who hear, in distant traffic's hum,
their lost gunners stalling home.

TRAVELLING FAIR

The rainbows of the fair span out to one
volcanic gleam, dancing on the chrome
of huge wheels at the field's edge, where a boy
with level head at chassis height looks on
to phantoms lit in corridors between
tow-bars, diesel giants and booths' back screens.
Trailer doors slip open, costumes flag,
cables throb and catch the dragging foot.

Between the guy ropes and the three card trick,
the whirling cars and street's more usual traffic,
on a playground's edge, safely at the wire
my self's old flame steadies and hangs fire.
No gesture shows his restless swings of mood
but some slight brush of hand to cheek. He broods
while classmates freeze wild gestures to a grim
ecstatic clench, hurled upon a rim.

More thoughtful or unsure, this shade whose proof
inflames me as I pass, well out of youth:
our shadows briefly merge on sides of trucks.
A dreamer, bad at games, coach-sick on trips,
compared to present company, he made
a Larkinesque study: but never plain afraid.
Now friends hug children of their own and ride,
this after dinner outing was designed

to let a childless, twice-divorced grown up see
the lighter side of families: pub and poetry
being my usual subversion. But fairs are camps
where all that's past seems tawdry, little changed:
still gimcrack, brash and grasping; and enjoyed
as keenly by these children as I am to avoid
prefiguring shadows. Clapped mechanics
swing us into mid-air, blaze like ricks.

POETRY IN SCHOOLS

In his raucous nest the teacher bawls
"Today it's Yeats!"
and scans the empty faces, empty drive;
the swan-less park where last year's leavers sulk.

      Why poetry?
              What else?
      What else could be
      a wrench in the day's mechanical span?
      The beautiful women bend to praise

but find none in the dozen yawns
and minds whose fictions loop like tape,
who fail to see how measured lines
could brave an orthodoxy's scorn,

or force the poet out beyond
their knowledge, and our own.
Even now odd verses bring
letters from home.

      'Dear Headmaster,
                    Must my son
      (who needs two B's to read for Law)
      be taught old men are paltry things,
      and trash about Byzantium ... ?'

GEOGRAPHY OF ILLUSION

America's somewhere I've never been,
but I know what's found at each extreme:

primly-appointed, liberal, white
New England is a watery chart
of causeway roads that skirt to wooden
chalets on sounds, where single women
struggle with cellos and sexual frustration.

But the skin-deep South is yellow as corn,
dry as a whistle that moans like a horn;

tracks beside levee roads, black shacks
where winsome men and savage hounds
lay back in the sweat of the midnight still,
and marry girls of sweet fourteen ...

England's the place I've always been:
Americans think each village a green

with inns and cottages fussy as lace.
Returned from my village pub, I write
these lines beneath beams, by light of logs.
And Americans, I think, are right:
but then again, so naive.

THE LIFE OF MIRRORS

In a fine and expensive mirror
the light of an elegant seaside town
lies slightly foxed, and through it swims
cornice wreaths and candle auras
of classical, vanished rooms

where unsensational ghosts
settle a periwig, try a look,
and the curled beauty half sees
a differently made up eye engross
her own with buyer's greed.

Among the gilt of mirrors
displayed at ease like showroomed cars
competing serenely in bland array
are patchworks of sea-light, Georgian pillars,
faces whose looks can pay.

The looks one sees behind glass
in glossy cars that flash across
the narrow mouths of damaged streets.
Sour lights caress their slipping past;
enfiladed, sleek,

deflecting envious praise.
In the sea-spacious town mirrors show
no traffic on steel-grey, plate-glazed ocean
only, in shallow time-softened daze,
a costly self-absorption,

a sort of private abstractedness,
plying its arcade of languid tastes
where a brick, unthinkably thrown, could net
great loss in a mesh of shards but miss
the world it never met.

COASTING

A land whose cargo packs in such tight space
so many creaking dreams of sea's brave face
should end triumphantly, the sea-starved find
their visions of the maritime full-flood:
vivid beaches, castled cliffs, old salt's
embracing havens, empire-serving ports.
Yet few roads run to more than scrub and dust;
the sea a dulled suggestion, but for rust
sharpening a trailing fence: the light
is oceanic but current is a feint
pulse among reeds, land ooze and plastic scrap.
The country gives out like a sinking map,
a deck split by storms, muddy-plimsoll lined.
It's last resorts are cheaply made and served:
the wooden cafe sweats its blinds of steam,
stale caravans in rows sag stem to stern.
It all corrodes, abrades, the blue-glass view
ebbs away inside the telescope's screw
through which we scan the roads, convenient flags
snap to attention, an aging moth-balled fleet
heaves on its chains, watched by a skeleton crew
whose wire-bloody bones skipper laughs fit to spew,
an arcade case whose dusty treasure chest
brims with tentacles from sea nightmare's nest.

AVERAGE RAINFALL

Sound track to the scene where she
twirls him under the fans, or an heir
returns to the island's disputatious
table, rain on the idle veranda
is a beaded percussive curtain, a sieve

too wild to drum all night, but eyes
lashed with glittering drops must turn
down sinking paths, too hot to wait
for a sheltered hour. The news floods out:
"She loves." "He's back." Dark banyans weep.

If rain in torrents underscores
at fever-pitch such passions flung
against the convention of sitting out
a roaring night, what inaction suits
the damp sulk that shuts in

this English house, upholstered lawns
plumped by a dull down-shading mood
of drizzling air? Interminable
staring out of phlegmatic days:
it might be dusk or dawn at noon.

Cattle digest and gain weight,
they are stopped clocks, untrodden paths
are overhung with still cranes
of gathering drops. A cistern whispers,
brimming a trough where no face peers,

there's no force but the gutter's plash,
the tick of a cracked pipe, damp
inching like cancer on dry stone.
We dream of tropical bursts and steam.
Letters from islands thirst for home.

WILD GEESE

An even numbered undulating rank,
more fluent than any victor's wing,
beats upstream in fluid air.

Slow strokes just keep plump breasts from stalling,
throats outstretched like runners at the tape
stutter in effort, chant or trance.

Or do trailing partners hector mates
always ahead: this reach is good as any,
doubting the lode in each goose skull

that draws them on unswervingly as sex?
Perhaps only one has Mosaic drive,
flogging on with flanking acolytes.

Evenly paced throughout the long valley,
banking and gone, they stick together;
paired in a mutual faith that might show love.

RABBIT DUSK

It matters to none why you appear,
calm sentinel of fields grown quiet;
what points of your lost life incline
or bind you to this vigilance.

It might be that your children came
habitually to this green hour.
Your knowledge of them is out of date,
and shadows fall too deep for play.

Your motions are feints, the gauzy light
could be the extension of pastoral thought:
though consciousness has ceased its beat
some watching thing is evening's author;

each slow refulgent diminishing
relates the perfection of summer dusk,
each 'nothing more' like a last clear sight;
were you not, though sighted, far beyond last.

At will as great as the brimming trees
or less than visible, ghost of a rabbit
silence the whistle on fools' lips,
until the stars come out like dogs.

THE WORLD THAT DAY

In populous wreckage
brute appetites gutter,
gorged on poisons.
Then an all comprehending quiet.
Even the most tame curl and hug their bones.

Earth like a mad face,
sky a chemist's swill
shot with livid
squalls that sting the river's hackles.
A butchered cry of loss, then sudden night.

No settlement made,
no party with word.
There was no sway
of wheat where sussurrant shadows smoothed
golden pages. Where this was written was ash.

VALEDICTION
'O love, subject of the mere diurnal grind,'
                    Geoffrey Hill, ANNUNCIATIONS.

Happiness I always saw too late; assayed
by memories, alloyed by time, and paid
as loss. "Were we happy?" Then I could not say.
Though now I can, you have no heart to stay.

from
NOT GETTING ON

NOT GETTING ON *is a loose collection of poems linked by a common theme, written in the space of a year. At the time of their writing it seemed that the portrayal of rural Britain as a comfortable and simple alternative to the cities was at its most intense. The images used to illustrate this neat and mellow fantasy world were very much at odds with many elements of rural life as I experienced it, living on the Mendip Hills in Somerset. Isolation, rural poverty and inherited disadvantage seemed too easily removed from the 'wonderful discoveries' of the property columns and from the golden images of country living that were endlessly presented as a consumer path back to a preservable Arcadia. These poems are an attempt to redress the balance: to include the mud, the chained dog and the unspeaking child in the littered farm yard.*

RUIN'S RACK

'(He) watched the rooks sweeping over the treetops and the great herds of sheep coming down from the grassy uplands to the folds in the valley. Suddenly he found himself filled "with wonder that a heart and mind so wrapped up in everything belonging to the gardens, the fields and the woods, should have been condemned to waste themselves away among the stench, the noise and the strife of cities ..."'

GEORGE WOODCOCK quoting WILLIAM COBBETT

'The country is where one doesn't get on.'
'The Poet', AKENFIELD

RUIN'S RACK

Ruin's rack draws to the bone;
frustrates ambition, wedlocks relations,
rattles old men in ramshackle yards
cursing at chickens, arthritic dogs,
at spinster sister's slaps of washing.
Old eyes are close as shot-gun bores.

Ruin's rack is stolen inches
stretched to a torture; boundaries chivvied
by incomers, councils, bungalow tenants.
A man might work in a stream all day
stringing wire so that differently owned
identical herds drink separate water.

Ruin's rack is the ribs showing through
where pantiles slip and wreck pulls rank.
Nettles grow best where there's things to hide:
a well-trap and chain, tines of tetanus;
a scullery window where coppers seethe
and flies grow hard on the nailed-shut pane.

'LEFT FOR THE SEA, RIGHT FOR THE LAND'

Nothing in earth speaks more of peace
than headstones in a grove of yews
open to fields where descendants keep
crops in the pattern of a patched old coat.
Names lie together like daisy heads,
but the sorrow is there, to any who know;
the missing familiars, those who quarrelled:
buried in sand, at sea; or unburied.
The elder sons who left before dawn
swept from rigging in their first typhoon;
blistered prospectors for copra and gum
who never sent word; yeoman recruits
bamboozled in kasbas, slit behind curtains,
drilled to advance at the proper pace
into air full of lead as hay-barn motes,
bearing to the utmost ends
some trace of the village boy and man.
Or somehow worse, those who returned
stripped of that trace, with foreign brides
and a fortune in stories;
galling brothers grown to the land,
cooking strange meals that fired great rows—
Who left one night, taken by devils,
leaving a parrot that echoed their name.

In somnolent parlours old women brood
on the ornaments of adventuring youth:
these silks, that beaten Moorish tray,
the lacquered dragons on a Chinese box;
the ringed face in a lost complement;
a nephew photographed with an ape.

A FAILED BUSINESS

Tenants slip away like crimes,
the stagnant farms, green and black,
are empty and peppered as tin.

Across small fields breaks a rare
new roof, the profit of learning
alien tastes; yet petering out

like a trickle of beer in the night:
soon only one van of three
in a damp yard can move itself;

and rain keeps close, a day-long soak;
and beads drip down, drunkenly told
"I'm not to blame ... No-one's to blame"

LANDLORD

When a man owns land
he must have care;
show little to strangers
but wariness.
Hard on his creatures,
thin with his children,
the years ahead
are bones to clothe.

As he curses the slow cows home
the college boy riding a combine
crosses his saturnine gaze—
Investment is reckless and garish.

The land is upheld,
preserved from invasion:
his dread of hunger
is sharper because
it is in the mouths
of those who depend
on his sly husbandry.
He dreams accusations.

    He does not hear those mouths
    whisper round the table;
    even his cattle fatten
    when they break onto neighbour's grass.

When a man has land
his nerves lie raw
over every inch;
scraped by the latch
of open trespass.
Vermin scuttle
through his rages
consuming whole ricks.

    Stamping in, he finds
    the note, the Rayburn cold;
    and every mild eye herded
    at his back is mocking him.

SHELTER

Water's simples, mud and ice,
can close the farm in a week:
this steady drench drives men and beasts
deeper into gloom and overhangs.

A day to trespass, an excuse to break
the seal of unwelcome this farm kept in life.

"Is this the room where he was found?"
Hard to imagine plaster falling
after the shot-gun's sudden bark:
bird-song resuming its innocent theme.

Feral creatures, soothed by rain,
range through nettle-carpeted barns.
Rubbing webs from the bedroom glass
I start at a figure stooped in the yard

a split sack over shoulders and a head
in the old manner, like a penitent.
I look again and see a coat
hung to wither on a rotten post.

They've gone, as clean as any tenant
who ever upped and left; gone by their own hand.
They have not the power to move one mote
in the too-long stifled air—

When from the barns a broken shriek
of agony snaps in a long-primed trap.

COUNTRY WAYS (1)

It is the ferrous spike that juts
from a lichened stem of flowing wood
in the dry aisles of the soughing wood,
that disconcerts like a ju-ju doll:

like distant metronomic blows
ghosting a wing clatter, driving home
a snag for the smooth arm, swinging home,
that trespasses on some rough grudge.

COUNTRY WAYS (2)

Good days like these are golden watches,
as round as coins, and running down
to a spent gleam, a charcoal sketch
of woods and a silhouette
cycling along the rim.

The hours are meals brought out of doors
to a garden of tiny Latin graves:
at dusk the latch on the hedgerow gate
jerks like a bolt in its breech.
Are these your supper guests?

No, it is the congregation,
moon-faced from keeping bull's-eyes lit
to steer raw fields to this calm bay.
They jostle blooms you cull for pleasure,
grasp your herbs by different, lethal names.

THE MODEL VILLAGE

The village store sold things
that only picture-book shops might stock:
sweets like planets, gypsy pegs,
china eggs for hens.

The bull's-eyed window held
a green, a Morris, the Church Row;
and houses I thought would cost the earth
where they still stood unmarked—

But here real village people
played village parts, or quietly raked
gardens not shaken by rushing trucks.
I eavesdropped on rustic speech,

civilities so pat
they might have been models from a guide
to casual discourse in some dated
gloss on etiquette.

And whether I'd stepped back
in some impossible, physical way,
or simply followed turnings far
enough from main roads' blight,

this place was special, this
was all those English novels laced
with green gentility made flesh
and blood, cob and tile.

Look, here are tweedy men
from the Big House; these cottagers
are all their tenants. There in the cockled
window, pale and stray

as a daylight moon, a face
authentically inbred. And here
come village women trailing their years
of children whose lives will be thus.

THE LAST HOUSE IN THE VILLAGE

Their tenancy is prolonged dispute;
bearing the oldest village name
but none of its freehold, they live at odds
like people cleared from altered land.
Unlikely gadgetry festoons
stained render with cable, wrecked once-
sumptuous cars are home to rot.

At the flat end of a small estate
their gate of pallet staves gives out;
garden a wilderness, where boys
try games with untried dogs.
All around lap level miles of crops
through which no rights of way play out,
imprisoning as city roads

for the full brood of children caught
in a shed door, a Victorian group
of siblings, depending and protective.
But their mothers are not shawled in silence;
on brisk stilettos, bare legged in frost
in the fashions of last year but one
they are erratic as their households:

windows sealed through summer, uncurtained
all winter, filled at any hour
with the swell and wash of television.
Daughters harden to small women early,
mothers are fools of their sparse youth.
They share habits, could swap clothes
and roles, and often do.

In the long summer twilights when
the myth of rural England almost
rises to the lip of saucered counties,
their television's cold blue storm,
the dog's unwanted bark, disrupt
the reverie of green-gold light
with historic dispossession.

COTTAGE

True home is timeless, unattainable;
full of past goods, intact, better than new:
the heart-shaped fretwork on the dresser's brow,
the sprigs of green that wreath imperfect glass.

Its spell and comfort is we do not know
what networks bind it to the days and tasks
of life beyond old brick and trees that cloak
such rights of way as thread the hanging wood.

Love peoples it, through inner doors half-heard
at other tasks; the moon-faced clock's most clear,
ticking any-century's constellations
across the chart above the gable end.

The fire curls in its basket, ginger cat;
stray draughts brush round the tails of outdoor coats
hung in shadow, like costumes in chilly wings—
That wreath might anchor Christmas or a loss.

POET IN THE GREEN ESTATE

It had fallen to this already
when a poet and his woman came
to the green care of a great estate
left for taxes and the spring riot
of drives turned back to cattle droves.

Windows, lens of dusty bottles,
grey on green above the yard
where lamp-eyed cars had been attended:
a horn of punctured mirror
glinted like remote chrome.

Nothing to do but write;
the rot too deep for maintenance,
only the bulk of the house ensured
a trickle of sustaining facts:
slates just holding, pipes gushing rust

to fill a bath designed to float
wives of ambassadors; corridors
linking unattended glooms
where codes and wire grew slack.
Old coats hung up their livery.

After the winter she left,
the poet's woman, steps bending
grass too long to be cut.
The poet watched his car decay,
smudged at the back of verdigrised shade,

used cold from lead when hot ran dry,
moved rooms as slates let ceilings drop
their tired laths. In time his words
were left unkempt to slip apart,
like silvered glass, to catch or not.

IN THE MUSHROOM WOOD

By tones the wood meshed in from bright
to deeper green; became an indoor place.
Saplings linked sharp branches, forced
the path to turn as neatly as a maze,
then fell back on a clearing where
straight rides led off as though through forest doors.
A ring of tumps, some vivid grass
composed the stage for a play where characters
convene at set hours in a glade
while action-off is relayed. No-one came.

Branch lines led to further mossy junctions;
familiar webs, differently viewed:
had we come round? We cut an Indian blaze—
It healed before we passed again.
The deep plantations grew so close and still
like cut-outs in a childrens' book,
a nightmare of musty card where pulling tags
turns boles to ogres, drooping boughs
to purple wings of beasts like pterodactyls.
The wood was full of metronomes.

With a fling like dice the shade was spotted blue,
green walls let in the light and breeze
of fields; we neared the rapids of a road.
We had not counted on the years
green minds must take to flesh out a design;
longer by far than any keeper
who lived to shut the brakes up like a snare;
longer than the gnomish woodman
of evergreen tales, whose heart-land is a strange
trompe l'oeil, a wood in a secret room.

FIELD SYSTEM

Summer tips its bowl of clouds,
its brim of china blue. Light
extends, and dry spells hold brief sway:
in verdant drought rich stems bend down.

Under prevailing threats hot farmers
roar all hours along the lane
hazed with diesel, dust and chaff.
A shuddering cab trembles light

on dazzled glass. Invaded fields
are combed unbroken to pattern and turn,
followed contours woven and swept—
Only clouds bloom on unkempt.

Twilight's curfew is overrun,
tractors paired in low gear prowl
behind each hedge. Uncut tides
shrink back, a trailer sways like a drunk

gaining the crown. I watch as the moon
gleans stubble to a silver matt;
and rain begins, like small lives
stirring to forage a poorer world.

GOATS

The butt of jokes,
my family additions:
two 'kids'; and me, twice married,
happily childless ...

Anecdotal beasts:
sappers of hedgerows,
with diabolical eyes
and appetites;

but mine from their first
milk-white days.
And in the full-blown,
sack-bellied, bellicose browsers

I see the just-born struggle
to bony knees, then miniature hoofs.
That the hearts of creatures mean less
than care between humans

(save to the old,
enfeebled and lonely)
I will not accept. But goats!
Too rank and simple for feeling.

And these, like kids,
at divorce were contested
and driven away.
Their banks are an emptied room.

Their absence grazes
and tethers the senses:
a wisp of pale smoke
is stretched to a neck,

a cry from the blue
becomes their own;
and summer's beard
has shot to seed.

THE LONELY GIRLS ON CHESTNUT HORSES

The lonely girls on chestnut horses
skirt the sunset and arterial roar
seductively relaxed astride
the bovine slouch of their mounts.

Home to what vacancies? Unwinding
clocks, petals on polished wood,
to mothers nervous that stable reek
is garlic in young mens' faces.

The silent girls in pink bathrooms
scrub horse ordure from their palms,
their thoughts secure as paddock gates
lounge like horses, feeding all night.

There seem so many in the long evenings
trotting correctly along the verges;
a moody cavalry raised in blameless
homes of mannered, well-spoken love.